WIT AND ACID

SHARP LINES FROM THE PLAYS OF
GEORGE BERNARD SHAW

VOLUME II

Wit and Acid

Sharp Lines from
the Plays of

GEORGE BERNARD SHAW

VOLUME II

selected by
SIMON MUNDY

RENARD PRESS

RENARD PRESS LTD

124 City Road
London EC1V 2NX
United Kingdom
info@renardpress.com
020 8050 2928

www.renardpress.com

Extracts taken from plays first published between 1914 and 1924
(for more information see original publication dates on p. 71)
This edition first published by Renard Press Ltd in 2023

Cover design by Will Dady

Printed in the United Kingdom by Severn

ISBN: 978-1-80447-068-8

9 8 7 6 5 4 3 2 1

CLIMATE POSITIVE Renard Press is proud to be a climate positive publisher, removing more carbon from the air than we emit and planting a small forest. For more information see renardpress.com/eco.

CONTENTS

INTRODUCTION

George Bernard Shaw (1856–1950) was a writer who plied his trade with an astounding volume and facility. He allowed his pen to carry on going with an ease that sometimes seems unstoppable. He wrote an awful lot of plays, containing an awful lot of words. He was a storyteller who loved the process of telling almost as much – perhaps more than – the story itself.

He loved to be contrary, and he lived long enough to irritate and charm several generations, first as a theatre and music critic and, from the 1890s, for forty years, as a playwright. He enjoyed being an outsider, whether in his early years as a Protestant in Dublin without a recognised father, or later in London as the scourge of social affectation and any form of lazy political posturing. He was a socialist who fell out with the Labour Party almost as soon as it was formed, an Irishman who disliked English rule but was equally suspicious of radical independence, particularly when beholden to the conservatism of the Catholic Church. He thought royalty ridiculous but republicanism inevitably corrupt, democracy necessary but bound to result in ill-thought-out policy and short-term populism. Although he was rude about his contemporaries, he was not afraid to poke fun at himself, either as a critic or playwright – as he does in *Fanny's First Play*.

This second volume of *Wit And Acid* covers plays written and performed during the period from 1910 to 1924, which was an extraordinary time to be a social and political commentator as war and revolution ripped apart the certainties of hierarchy and imperialism. Shaw responded with barbed scepticism. In 1910 the flamboyant and amiable Edward VII was on his way out, to be succeeded on the British and Imperial throne by his stiff, dull and unimaginative son George V. In government the Conservatives had been replaced by the Liberals, led by the mild Yorkshireman, Herbert Asquith, and his Welsh fire-and-brimstone Chancellor of the Exchequer, David Lloyd George. Between them they introduced income taxes for the rich, pensions for the old and limited the powers of the hereditary House of Lords. King George was told to mind his own business and effectively became a salaried employee of the state (though it was dressed up as a settlement called the Civil List). He got to live in his palaces and castles, but not to own them, except his grandmother's big hunting lodge at Balmoral. Then the First World War, surely one of the most pointless conflicts in a long history of those, led to the downfall of the Russian, German, Ottoman and Austro-Hungarian emperors. By 1924 the Conservatives were back in power in Britain and the once-formidable Liberal Party had split between its economic and social wings. Lloyd George, after ousting Asquith and being defeated by Stanley Baldwin, had compromised himself into irrelevance by keeping the Tories in power long after it was necessary, as Nick Clegg was to do with similar results ninety years later.

Shaw's plays chronicle the progression. Those from before the outbreak of war lambast and lampoon English class divisions and social pomposity, as well as the nonsensical conventions keeping women trapped by dependence on the one hand and insincere delicacy on the other:

glorified but not respected. The plays take plots to ridiculous conclusions, and are very funny in the process. His satire extends mercilessly into the first years of war as such conventions are – literally, in one play, *Heartbreak House* – blown apart. He unpicks political contradictions and pours scorn on everyone's patriotic motives, whether in England, Ireland or in a succession of fictional countries invented to mimic the futility of European royalty.

Sometimes his moodiness and despair at human folly leads him to write at length well beyond the endurance of any theatre audience. His survey of life from the Garden of Eden to the end of the world, *Back to Methuselah*, abandons all constraint. I am only slightly ashamed to have reduced its thousands of lines to a brief exchange between Adam and the serpent; a mild in-joke which I hope readers will forgive.

One of the wittiest of Shaw's satirical pieces is *Annajanska, the Bolshevik Empress*, which pokes fun at all the old Imperial bureaucrats who suddenly had to serve new regimes after the collapse of the Ottoman, Austro-Hungarian and Tsarist Empires. How are they expected to manage when there is no accepted government to serve, and how should they address a Grand Duchess who has swapped sides, either from conviction or expediency, and joined the revolution? All the familiar themes of Shaw's work are at play: a strong female character making nonsense of male political certainties, confused men trying to maintain their conventional dignity as both the conventions and their dignity are rendered pointless, the fragile absurdity of social hierarchy, and an understanding of the sheer banality of most governments. Throughout this small volume I have selected lines because they are either still funny, apt, or say something unchanging about our era as much as Shaw's.

Readers will be driven mad by his eccentric spelling and punctuation, especially his refusal to put a final 'e' on Shakespear and his determination not to use an apostrophe in any normal setting. Perhaps he was harking back to the flexibility of seventeenth and eighteenth-century usage; perhaps he just wanted to annoy his editors and proofreaders; or, most likely, he just felt like being difficult and disguising his whim as conviction. Either way, I have given in and adhered to his versions.

SIMON MUNDY

2023

WIT AND ACID

MISALLIANCE

JOHNNY TARLETON, *an ordinary young business man of thirty or less, is taking his weekly Friday to Tuesday in the house of his father,* JOHN TARLETON, *who has made a great deal of money out of Tarleton's Underwear. The house is in Surrey, on the slope of Hindhead; and* JOHNNY, *reclining, novel in hand, in a swinging chair with a little awning above it, is enshrined in a spacious half-hemisphere of glass which forms a pavilion commanding the garden… The glass pavilion springs from a bridgelike arch in the wall of the house, through which one comes into a big hall with tiled flooring, which suggests that the proprietor's notion of domestic luxury is founded on the lounges of weekend hotels.*

BENTLEY: I was probably unintentional. My brothers and sisters are not the least like me. Theyre the regular thing that

15

you always get in the first batch from young parents: quite pleasant, ordinary, do-the-regular-thing sort: all body and no brains, like you.

JOHNNY: Thank you.

BENTLEY: Dont mention it, old chap. Now I'm different. By the time I was born ye old couple knew something. So I came out all brains and no more body than is absolutely necessary.

*

BENTLEY: Ive read it. 'The Romance of Business, or The Story of Tarleton's Underwear. Please Take One!' I took one the day after I first met Hypatia. I went and bought half a dozen unshrinkable vests for her sake.

JOHNNY: Well: did they shrink?

BENTLEY: Oh, dont be a fool.

JOHNNY: Never mind whether I'm a fool or not. Did they shrink? Thats the point. Were they worth the money?

BENTLEY: I couldnt wear them: do you think my skin's as thick as your customers' hides? I'd as soon have dressed in a nutmeg grater.

*

LORD SUMMERHAYS: Bentley is a problem which I confess I have never been able to solve. He was born to be a great success at the age of fifty. Most Englishmen of his class seem to be great successes at the age of twenty-four at most. The domestic problem for me is how to endure Bentley until he is fifty. The problem for the nation is how to get itself governed by men whose growth is arrested when they are little more than college lads.

*

BENTLEY: The dear old son is always telephoning or telegraphing: he thinks hes hustling along like anything when hes only sending unnecessary messages.

*

MRS TARLETON: I used to think that the aristocracy were a nasty sneering lot… Theyre always giggling and pretending not to care much about anything. But you get used to it: theyre the same to one another and to everybody. Besides, what does it matter what they think? It's far worse when theyre civil, because that always means they want you to lend them money; and you must never do that, Hypatia, because they never pay. How can they? They dont make anything, you see.

*

MRS TARLETON: [Bentley's] overbred, like one of those little dogs. I like a bit of a mongrel myself, whether it's a man or a dog: theyre best for everyday.

*

TARLETON: They talk of the wickedness and vanity of women painting their faces and wearing auburn wigs at fifty. But why shouldnt they? Why should a woman allow Nature to put a false mask of age on her when she knows she's as young as ever? …The wrinkles are a dodge to repel young men. Suppose she doesnt want to repel young men! Suppose she likes them!

MRS TARLETON: Bunny: take Hypatia out into the grounds for a walk, theres a good boy. John has got one of his naughty fits this evening.

*

TARLETON: We want to be governed here in England. Govern us.

LORD SUMMERHAYS: Here everything has to be done the wrong way, to suit governors who understand nothing but partridge shooting (our English native princes, in fact) and voters who dont know what theyre voting about. I dont understand these democratic games; and I'm afraid I'm too old to learn. What can I do but sit in the window of my club, which consists mostly of retired Indian civil servants? We look at the muddle and folly and amateurishness; and we ask each other where a single fortnight would have landed us... Democracy reads well; but it doesnt act well, like some people's plays.

*

JOHNNY: You look on an author as a sort of god. *I* look on him as a man that I pay to do a certain thing for me. I pay him to amuse me and to take me out of myself and make me forget... If I find that the author's getting at me the whole time, I consider that he's obtained my money under false pretences... The time has come for sane, healthy, unpretending men like me to make a stand against this conspiracy of the writing and talking and artistic lot to put us in the back row.

*

TARLETON: In the theatre of life everyone may be amused except the actor.

*

HYPATIA: If parents would only realize how they bore their children! Three or four times in the last half hour Ive been on the point of screaming... I'm fed up with nice things: with respectability, with propriety! When a woman has nothing to do, money and respectability mean that nothing is ever allowed to happen to her. I dont want to be good; and I dont want to be bad... I want to be an active verb.

*

TARLETON: Look at what the Romans did for Britain! ...They were the making of us... That's the good side of Imperialism: it's unselfish. I despise the Little Englanders:

theyre always thinking about England. Smallminded. I'm for the Parliament of man, the federation of the world. Read Tennyson.

*

TARLETON: I'm a married man, not a widower like you. A married man can do anything he likes if his wife dont mind. A widower cant be too careful.

*

LINA: Common people do not pray, my lord: they only beg.

*

GUNNER: The greatness of a poet is the greatness of his greatest moment. Shakespear used to get drunk. Frederick the Great ran away from a battle. But it was what they could rise to, not what they could sink to, that made them great.

*

LORD SUMMERHAYS: Men are not governed by justice, but by law or persuasion. When they refuse to be governed by law or persuasion, they have to be governed by force or fraud, or both… anarchism is a game at which the police can beat you.

*

PERCIVAL: [The priest] assures me that if marriages were made by putting all the men's names into one sack and the women's names into another, and having them taken out by a blindfolded child like lottery numbers, there would be just as high a percentage of happy marriages as we have here in England.

*

LINA: All you have to say is to ask me not to mention that you made love to me in Vienna two years ago. I forgave you because I thought you were an ambassador; and all ambassadors make love and are very nice and useful to people who travel.

THE DARK LADY OF THE
SONNETS

THE LADY: You talk too much, sir. Let me warn
you: I am more accustomed to be listened
to than preached at.

*

QUEEN ELIZABETH: And who in the name of
all the sluts and jades and light-o'-loves and
fly-by-nights that infect this palace of mine
may William Shakespear be?

*

SHAKESPEAR: You are no true Tudor: this
baggage here has as good a right to your
royal seat as you. What maintains you on
the throne of England? Is it your renownéd

23

wit? Your wisdom that sets at nought the craftiest statesmen of the Christian world? No. Tis the mere chance that might have happened to any milkmaid, the caprice of Nature that made you the most wondrous piece of beauty the age has seen. That is what hath brought all men to your feet, and founded your throne on the impregnable rock of your proud heat, a stony island in a sea of desire.

ELIZABETH (*with dignity*): Master Shakespear... remember that there are things that be true, and are yet not seemly to be said...

THE DARK LADY: He hath ever some lewd jest on his tongue. You hear how he useth me!

*

SHAKESPEAR: Oh, madam, can I go about with the modest cough of a minor poet, belittling my inspiration and making the mightiest wonder of your reign a thing of nought? I have said that 'not marble nor the gilded monuments of princes shall outlive' the words with which I make the world glorious or foolish at my will.

*

SHAKESPEAR: The boon I crave is that you endow a great playhouse, or, if I may make bold to coin a scholarly name for it, a National Theatre, for the better instruction and gracing of your Majesty's subjects.

ELIZABETH: Why, sir, are there not theatres enow on the Bankside and in Blackfriars?

SHAKESPEAR: Madam: these are the adventures of needy and desperate men that must, to save themselves from perishing of want, give the sillier sort of people what they best like… Wherefore I humbly beg your Majesty to give order that a theatre be endowed out of the public revenue for the playing of those pieces of mine which no merchant will touch… For this writing of plays is a great matter, forming as it does the minds and affections of men in such sort that, whatsoever they see done in show on the stage, they will presently be done in earnest in the world, which is but a larger stage…

ELIZABETH: Master Shakespear: I will speak of this matter to the Lord Treasurer.

SHAKESPEAR: Then I am undone, madam; for there was never yet a Lord Treasurer that could find a penny for anything over and above the necessary expenses of your government, save for a war or a salary for his own nephew.

ELIZABETH: It will be three hundred years and more before my subjects learn that man cannot live by bread alone... Until every other country in the Christian world, even to barbarian Muscovy and the hamlets of the boorish Germans, have its playhouse at the public charge, England will never adventure... But this I will say: that if I could speak across the ages to our descendants, I should heartily recommend them to fulfil your wish; for the Scottish minstrel hath well said that he that maketh the songs of a nation is mightier than he that maketh its laws.

This little scene (by Shaw's standards) is one of the early attempts to stimulate public funding for the arts in Britain and the founding of a National Theatre. Maybe he thought that with David Lloyd George as the Liberal Chancellor of the Exchequer and the theatre-loving (or at least actress-loving) Edward VII on the throne, and the Asquith family in 10 Downing Street, there was a chance of at least matching Vienna and Prague. Sadly, Edward was soon dead, the First World War ruined everything, and it was another fifty years before Peter Hall and Lawrence Olivier managed to persuade the government, via the Arts Council of Great Britain, to establish and fund the Royal Shakespeare Company and the National Theatre. Wales and Scotland had to wait a further forty years or more for theirs.

FANNY'S FIRST PLAY

An Easy Play for a Little Theatre

THE COUNT: The difficulty is not that there are no beautiful realities: the difficulty is that so few of us know them when we see them.

INDUCTION

*

THE COUNT: The century I shut out will always be the nineteenth century... I found England befouled with industrialism... I did what Byron did: I simply refused to live in it... I find England ugly and Philistine. I find modern houses ugly. I dont live in them: I have a palace on the Grand Canal... I find Beethoven's music coarse and restless, and

Wagner's senseless and detestable... You can imagine how we feel here.

SAVOYARD: Rather out of it, eh?...

THE COUNT: Out of soot and fog and mud and east wind; out of vulgarity and ugliness, hypocrisy and greed, superstition and stupidity...

SAVOYARD: Some of us must live in England, you know, just to keep the place going.

INDUCTION

*

SAVOYARD: You must be careful what you say about that: I shouldnt like anyone to call me an Intellectual: I dont think any Englishman would! They dont count, really, you know; but still it's rather the thing to have them.

INDUCTION

*

FANNY: [My father] never gives way on a point of art. I darent let him know that I love Beethoven and Wagner; and as to Strauss, if he heard three bars of Elektra, it'd part us for ever.

INDUCTION

*

TROTTER (A CRITIC): Ive lived a blameless life. Ive supported the Censorship in the face of ridicule and insult. And now I'm told that I'm a centre of Immoralism! Of Modern Minxism! A trifler with the most sacred subjects! A Nietzschean!! Perhaps a Shavian!!!

INDUCTION

*

DUVALLET: (*He speaks English better... having learnt it on both sides of the Atlantic.*)

ACT II

*

MARGARET: You shouldnt have prayed for me to be enlightened if you didnt want me to be enlightened. If the truth were known, I suspect we all want our prayers to be answered only by halves: the agreeable halves.

ACT II

*

MRS KNOX: I do say that when people have happiness within themselves, all the earthquakes, all the floods and all the prisons in the world cant make them really unhappy.

ACT III

*

BANNAL: Who would you say [the play's] by, Gunn?…

GUNN: The naval lieutenant is a Frenchman who cracks up the English and runs down the French: the hackneyed old Shaw touch. The characters are second-rate middle class, instead of being dukes or millionaires. The heroine gets kicked through the mud: real mud. Theres no plot. All the old stage conventions and puppets without the old ingenuity and the old enjoyment. And a feeble air of intellectual pretentiousness kept up all through… Why, the play bears the author's signature in every line… Granville-Barker, of course…

BANNAL: Poor old Barker!…

VAUGHAN: To begin with, it's intensely disagreeable. Therefore it's not by Barrie, in spite of the footman…

BANNAL: I believe it's Shaw.

GUNN: Rubbish!

VAUGHAN: Poor as this play is, there's a note of passion in it… Now Ive repeatedly proved that Shaw is physiologically incapable of the note of passion.

BANNAL: Yes, I know. Intellect without emotion. Thats right. I always say that myself. A giant brain, if you ask me; but no heart…

VAUGHAN: Well, at all events, you cant deny that the characters in this play are quite distinguishable from one another. That proves it's not by Shaw, because all Shaw's characters are himself: mere puppets stuck up to spout Shaw. It's only the actors that make them seem different.

BANNAL: There can be no doubt of that: everybody knows it. But Shaw doesnt write his plays as plays. All he wants to do is to insult everybody all round and set us talking about him.

TROTTER (*wearily*): And naturally, here we are all talking about him. For heaven's sake, let us change the subject.

VAUGHAN: Still, my articles about Shaw…

BANNAL: There you go, Shaw, Shaw, Shaw! Do chuck it.

EPILOGUE

ANDROCLES AND THE LION

My martyrs are the martyrs of all time and my persecutors the persecutors of all time. My Emperor, who has no sense of the value of common people's lives, and amuses himself with killing as carelessly as with sparing, is the sort of monster you can make of any silly-clever gentleman by idolizing him... But the most striking aspect of the play at this moment is the terrible topicality given it by war... If the Government decided to throw persons of unpopular or eccentric views to the lions in the Albert Hall or the Earl's Court stadium tomorrow, can you doubt that all the seats would be crammed, mostly by people who could not give you the most superficial account of the views in question? Much less unlikely things have happened...

It was currently reported in the Berlin newspapers that when Androcles was first performed in Berlin, the Crown Prince rose and left the house, unable to endure the (I hope) very clear and fair exposition of autocratic Imperialism given by the Roman captain to the Christian prisoners. No English Imperialist was intelligent and earnest enough to do the same in London. If the report is correct, I confirm the logic of the Crown Prince, and am glad to find myself so well understood. But I can assure him that the Empire which served for my model when I wrote Androcles was, as he is now finding to his cost, much nearer my home than the German one.

AFTERWORD,
ADDED DURING WWI

OVERRULED

GREGORY LUNN: I am surrounded with women who are most dear to me. But every one of them has a post sticking up, if I may put it that way, with the inscription: Trespassers Will Be Prosecuted. How we all loathe that notice! In every lovely garden, in every dell full of primroses, on every fair hillside, we meet that confounded board; and there is always a gamekeeper round the corner...

MRS JUNO: Wasnt there a widow?

GREGORY: No. Widows are extraordinarily scarce in modern society. Husbands live longer than they used to; and even when they do die, their widows have a string of names down for their next.

*

JUNO: You've guessed, of course, that I'm a married man.

MRS LUNN: Oh, that's all right. I'm a married woman.

JUNO: Thank Heavens for that! To my English mind, passion is not real passion without guilt... Marriage is all very well; but it isnt romance. Theres nothing wrong in it, you see...

MRS LUNN: Gregory has an idea that married women keep lists of the men they'll marry if they become widows. I'll put your name down, if that will satisfy you.

*

JUNO: Do you think a man's heart is a potato? Or a turnip? Or a ball of knitting wool? That you can throw it away like this?

MRS LUNN: I dont throw away balls of wool. A man's heart seems to me much like a sponge: it sops up dirty water as well as clean.

*

MRS LUNN: Here's a flower. Go and dream over it until you feel hungry. Nothing brings people to their senses like hunger.

*

MRS LUNN: Gregory is one of those terribly uxorious men who ought to have ten wives. If any really nice woman will take him off my hands for a day or two occasionally, I shall be greatly obliged to her.

*

MRS JUNO: Am I to speak only to men who dislike me?

JUNO: Yes: I think that is, properly speaking, a married woman's duty.

PYGMALION

THE NOTE TAKER (HENRY HIGGINS): You see this creature with her kerbstone English… in three months I could pass that girl off as a duchess at an ambassador's garden party. I could even get her a place as a lady's maid or shop assistant, which requires better English.

ACT I

*

HIGGINS: What is life but a series of inspired follies? The difficulty is to find them to do.

ACT II

*

MRS PEARCE: It's not right. She should think of the future.

HIGGINS: At her age? Nonsense! Time enough to think of the future when you havent any future to think of. No, Eliza: do as this lady does: think of other people's futures; but never think of your own. Think of chocolates, and taxis, and gold, and diamonds.

ACT II

*

HIGGINS: Do any of us understand what we are doing? If we did, would we ever do it?

ACT II

*

DOOLITTLE: I'm one of the underserving poor: that's what I am… up agen middle-class morality all the time… They charge me just the same as the deserving. What is middle-class morality? Just an excuse for never giving me anything.

ACT II

*

DOOLITTLE: Ten pounds is a lot of money; it makes a man feel prudent like; and then goodbye to happiness.

ACT II

*

DOOLITTLE: A year ago I hadnt a relative in the world except two or three that wouldnt speak to me. Now Ive fifty, and not a decent week's wages among the lot of them. I have to live for others and not for myself: that's middle-class morality.

ACT V

*

HIGGINS: The great secret, Eliza, is not having bad manners or any other particular sort of manners, but having the same manner for all human souls... The question is not whether I treat you rudely, but whether you ever heard me treat anyone else better...

LIZA: I won't care for anybody that doesnt care for me.

ACT V

*

HIGGINS: Commercial principles, Eliza... Independence? That's middle-class blasphemy. We are all dependent on one another, every soul of us on earth.

ACT V

*

[Eliza's] shop is in the arcade of a railway station not very far from the Victoria and Albert Museum; and if you live in that neighbourhood you may go there any day and buy a buttonhole from Eliza.

AFTERWORD

HEARTBREAK HOUSE

A Fantasia in the Russian Manner on English Themes

THE CAPTAIN: I have a second daughter who is, thank God, in a remote part of the Empire with her numbskull of a husband. As a child she thought the figurehead of my ship, the Dauntless, the most beautiful thing on earth. He resembled it. He had the same expression: wooden yet enterprising.

ACT I

*

ELLIE: How can you love a liar?
MRS HUSHABYE: I dont know. But you can, fortunately. Otherwise there wouldnt be much love in the world.

ACT I

*

ELLIE: If we women were particular about men's characters, we should never get married at all.

ACT II

*

MAZZANI: I'm afraid all the captains of industry are what you call frauds… Of course there are some manufacturers who really do understand their own works; but they dont make as high a rate of profit.

ACT II

*

ELLIE: This gentleman wants to know, is he never to have the last word?

LADY UTTERWORD: I should let him have it, my dear. The important thing is not to have the last word, but to have your own way.

MANGAN: She wants both.

LADY UTTERWORD: She wont get them, Mr Mangan. Providence always has the last word.

ACT II

*

MANGAN: In this house a man's mind might as well be a football. I'm going.

ACT II

*

ELLIE: Do you think I should marry Mr Mangan?

THE CAPTAIN: One rock is as good as another to be wrecked on.

ACT II

*

ELLIE: Old-fashioned people think you can have a soul without money. They think the less money you have the more soul you have. Yong people nowadays know better. A soul is a very expensive thing to keep: much more so than a motor car.

ACT II

*

THE CAPTAIN: A man's interest is only the overflow from his interest in himself. When you are a child your vessel is not yet full; so you care for nothing but your own affairs. When you grow up, your vessel overflows;

and you are a politician, a philosopher, or an explorer and adventurer. In old age the vessel dries up: there is no overflow: you are a child again.

ACT II

*

LADY UTTERWORD: There are only two classes of people in good society in England: the equestrian classes and the neurotic classes.

ACT III

*

MAZZANI: Every year I expected a revolution or some frightful smash-up: it seemed impossible that we could blunder and muddle on any longer. But nothing happened, except, of course, the usual poverty and crime and drink that we are used to. Nothing ever does happen.

ACT III

GREAT CATHERINE

Whom Glory Still Adores

PATIOMKIN: Young man: it is not better to be drunk than sober; but it is happier. Goodness is not happiness.

*

EDSTASTON: I am a Bachelor of Arts.

PATIOMKIN: It is enough that you are a bachelor, darling. Catherine will supply the arts.

*

PATIOMKIN: In Russia we face facts.

EDSTASTON: In England, sir, a gentleman never faces any facts if they are unpleasant facts.

PATIOMKIN: In real life, darling, all facts are unpleasant.

*

CATHERINE: You should know by this time that I am frank and original in character, like an Englishman... No: what maddens me about all this ceremony is that I am the only person in Russia who gets no fun out of my being Empress. You all glory in me: you bask in my smiles: you get titles and honors and favors from me: you are dazzled by my crown and my robes: you feel splendid when you have been admitted to my prescence; and when I say a gracious word to you, you talk about it to everyone you meet for a week afterwards. But what do I get out of it? Nothing... Nothing!! I wear a crown until my neck aches: I stand looking majestic until I am ready to drop: I have to smile at ugly old ambassadors and frown and turn my back on young and handsome ones. Nobody gives me anything... When I have headaches and colics I envy the scullerymaids... Let me tell you I would not give a rouble to have the brains of all the philosophers in France.

O'FLAHERTY V.C.

A Recruiting Pamphlet

SIR PEARSE: Does patriotism mean nothing to
 you?

O'FLAHERTY: It means different things to me
 than it would mean to you, sir. It means
 England and England's king to you. To me
 and the like of me, it means talking about
 the English just the way the English papers
 talk about the Boshes. And what good has
 it ever done here in Ireland? ...It's kept
 Ireland poor, because instead of trying to
 better ourselves we thought we was the fine
 fellows of patriots when we were speaking
 evil of Englishmen that was as poor as
 ourselves and maybe as good as ourselves.
 The Boshes I kilt was more knowledgeable

men than me: and what better am I now that Ive kilt them? What better is anybody?

*

O'FLAHERTY: What use is all the lying, and pretending, and humbugging, and letting on, when the day comes to you that your comrade is killed in the trench beside you, and you dont as much look round at him until you trip over his poor body, and then all you say is to ask why the hell the stretcher-bearers dont take it out of the way... Dont talk to me or any soldier of the war being right. No war is right: and all the holy water that Father Quinlan ever blessed couldnt make one right.

*

SIR PEARCE: Oh yes: we all have to think seriously sometimes, especially when we're a little run down. I'm afraid weve been overworking you a bit... However, we can knock off for the rest of the day; and tomorrow's Sunday. Ive had about as much as I can stand myself... It's tea-time... Really, O'Flaherty, the war seems to have upset you a little.

*

O'FLAHERTY: [My mother] says all the English generals is Irish. She says all the English poets and great men was Irish. She says the English never knew how to read their own books until we taught them. She says we're the lost tribes of the house of Israel and the chosen people of God. She says that the goddess Venus, that was born out of the foam of the sea, came up out of the water in Killiney Bay off Bray Head. She says that Moses built the seven churches, and that Lazarus was buried in Glasnevin.

*

O'FLAHERTY: [The English] never thought of being patriotic until the war broke out; and now the patriotism has took them so sudden and come so strange to them that they run about like frightened chickens, uttering all manner of nonsense... They think theres no one like themselves. It's the same with the Germans, though theyre educated and ought to know better. Youll never have a quiet world til you knock the patriotism out of the human race.

*

O'FLAHERTY: It's in the nature of governments to tell lies.

*

MRS O'FLAHERTY: Oh sir, I'm ruined and destroyed... He wants to marry a Frenchwoman on me, and to go away and be a foreigner and desert his mother and betray his country. It's mad he is with the roaring of the cannons and he killing the Germans and the Germans killing him, bad cess to them!

O'FLAHERTY: Who's going to leave you? I'm going to take you with me. There now: does that satisfy you?

MRS O'FLAHERTY: Is it take me into a strange land among heathens and pagans and savages... Ask me to die out of Ireland, is it? and the angels not to find me when they come for me!

*

SIR PEARSE [*after a furious battle between O'Flaherty's mother and girlfriend*]: Strictly between ourselves, and as one soldier to another, do you think we should have got an army without conscription if domestic life had been as happy a people say it is?

THE INCA OF PERUSALEM

An Almost Historical Comedietta

THE INCA: The Inca's moustache is so watched and studied that it has made his face the barometer of the whole continent. When that moustache goes up, culture rises with it. Not what you would call culture; but Kultur, a word so much more significant that I hardly understand it myself, except when I am in exceptionally good form. When it goes down, millions of my men perish.

*

THE INCA: What is sanity? The condition of the Inca's mind. What is madness? The condition of the people who disagree with the Inca.

*

ERMYNTRUDE: You want me to marry one of the Inca's sons: I forget which.

THE INCA: As far as I can recollect the name, it is His Imperial Highness Prince Eitel William Frederick George Franz Josef Alexander Nicholas Victor Emmanuel Albert Theodore Wilson...

ERMYNTRUDE: Oh, please, maynt I have one with a shorter name? What is he called at home?

THE INCA: He is usually called Sonny...

ERMYNTRUDE: Are [the Inca's sons] all as clever and charming as their father?

THE INCA: Pongo imitates farmyard sounds – cock-crowing and that sort of thing – extremely well. Lulu plays Strauss's Sinfonia Domestica on the mouth organ really screamingly. Chips keeps owls and rabbits... The Piffler writes plays, and paints most abominably. Yes they all have their different little talents.

*

THE INCA: Can you name a single man in the entourage of the Inca who is not a born fool?...

ERMYNTRUDE: If all the Inca's generals are incapables, and all his relatives duffers, Perusalem will be beaten in the war; and then it will become a republic, like France after 1871, and the Inca will be sent to St Helena.

THE INCA: That is just what the Inca is playing for, madam. It is why he consented to the war… Napoleon lacked versatility. After all, any fool can be a soldier: we know that only too well in Perusalem, where every fool is a soldier. But the Inca has a thousand other resources. He is an architect… He is a painter: need I remind you that St Helena is still without a National Gallery? Napoleon left no symphonies in St Helena. Send the Inca to St Helena, madam, and the world will crowd thither to see his works as they crowd now to Athens to see the Acropolis, to Madrid to see the pictures of Velasquez, to Bayreuth to see the music dramas of that egotistical old rebel Richard Wagner, who ought to have been shot before he was forty and very nearly was.

*

THE INCA: Give the people voting papers: good long voting papers, American fashion; and while the people are reading the voting papers the Government does what it likes.

*

THE INCA: You talk of death as an unpopular thing. You are wrong: for years I gave [my people] art, literature, science, prosperity, that they might live more abundantly; and they hated me, ridiculed me, caricatured me. Now that I give them death in its frightfullest forms, they are devoted to me. If you doubt me, ask those who for years have begged our taxpayers in vain for a few paltry thousands to spend on Life: on the bodies and minds of the nation's children, on the beauty and healthfulness of its cities, on the honor and comfort of its worn-out workers. They refused; and because they refused, death is let loose on them.

AUGUSTUS DOES HIS BIT

AUGUSTUS: Our statesmen are the greatest known to history. Our generals are invincible. Our army is the admiration of the world... How dare you tell me that the country is going to the dogs?

*

AUGUSTUS: The allowance of petrol has been reduced by three quarters?

THE CLERK: It has.

AUGUSTUS: And you have told the motor-car people to come here and arrange to start munition work?...

THE CLERK: It aint stopped. Theyre busier than ever.

AUGUSTUS: Busy at what?

THE CLERK: Making small cars... The old cars only do twelve miles to the gallon. Everybody has to have a car that will do thirty-five now.

AUGUSTUS: Cant they take the train?

THE CLERK: There aint no trains now. Theyve torn up the rails and sent them to the front.

*

AUGUSTUS (*taking up the telephone receiver*): What?... A spy!... A woman!... Yes, I brought it down with me. Do you suppose I'm such a fool as to let it out of my hands? Why, it gives a list of all our anti-aircraft emplacements from Ramsgate to Skegness... But how could she possibly know about it? I havent mentioned it to a soul, except, of course, dear Lucy... Oh, Toto and Lady Popham and that lot: they dont count: theyre all right.

*

AUGUSTUS: It would be strange indeed, if, after sitting on thirty-seven royal commissions, mostly as chairman, I had not mastered the art of public expression. Even the radical papers have paid me the high compliment of declaring that I am never more impressive than when I have nothing to say.

*

AUGUSTUS: A shot from our front trench struck me in the head. I still carry the flattened projectile as a trophy. Had it penetrated to the brain I might never have sat on another Royal commission. Fortunately we have strong heads, we Highcastles. Nothing has ever penetrated to our brains.

*

AUGUSTUS: Our people have for some reason made up their minds that the German War Office is everything that our War Office is not – that it carries promptitude, efficiency and organization to a pitch of completeness and perfection that must be, in my opinion, destructive to the happiness of the staff.

*

AUGUSTUS: The great advantage of being at war, madam, is that nobody takes the slightest notice of the House of Commons.

*

AUGUSTUS: I shall not permit it. What do they mean by taking my office staff? Good God! they'll be taking our hunt servants next.

*

AUGUSTUS: Excuse my violence; but discipline is absolutely necessary in dealing with the lower-middle classes... Believe me, you may waste a pound to save a penny; you may let out all sorts of secrets to the enemy; you may guide the zeppelins right on to your own chimneys. That's where the ability of the governing class comes in.

*

AUGUSTUS: You mean it was a real gun, and actually went off. How sad! How sad!

THE LADY: And now, Lord Augustus, I have taken up too much of your valuable time...

AUGUSTUS: What! Must you go?

THE LADY: You are so busy.

AUGUSTUS: Yes: but not before lunch, you know. I never can do much before lunch. And I'm no good at all in the afternoon. From five to six is my real working time.

ANNAJANSKA, THE BOLSHEVIK EMPRESS

A Revolutionary Romancelet

STRAMMFEST: Have you sent my report yet to the government?

SCHNEIDERKIND: Not yet, sir. Which government do you wish it sent to?

STRAMMFEST: That depends... Which of them do you think is most likely to be in power tomorrow morning?

SCHNEIDERKIND: Well, the provisional government was going strong yesterday. But today they say the Prime Minister has shot himself and that the extreme-left fellow has shot all the others... I should send the report to the Maximilianists.

STRAMMFEST: Theyre no stronger than the Oppidoshavians; and in my own opinion the Moderate Red Revolutionaries are as likely to come out on top as either of them.

SCHNEIDERKIND: I can easily put a few carbon sheets in the typewriter and send a copy each to the lot.

STRAMMFEST: Waste of paper. You might as well send reports to an infant school.

*

STRAMMFEST: Your Imperial Highness desires me to address you as comrade?

THE GRAND DUCHESS: Long live the Revolution, comrade!

STRAMMFEST: Proletarians of all lands, unite. Lieutenant Schneiderkind: you will rise and sing the Marseillaise.

SCHNEIDERKIND: But I cannot, sir. I have no voice, no ear.

STRAMMFEST: Then sit down; and bury your shame in your typewriter.

BACK TO METHUSELAH

THE SERPENT: Imagination is the beginning of creation. You imagine what you desire; you will what you imagine; and at last you create what you will.

PART I, ACT I

*

ADAM: Make me a beautiful word for doing things tomorrow; for that surely is a great and blessed invention.

THE SERPENT: Procrastination.

EVE: That is a sweet word.

PART I, ACT I

SAINT JOAN

THE ARCHBISHOP: There is a new spirit rising
in men: we are at the dawning of a wider
epoch. If I were a simple monk, and had
not to rule men, I should seek peace for my
spirit with Aristotle and Pythagoras rather
than with the saints and their miracles.

*

JOAN: Minding your own business is like
minding your own body: it's the shortest
way to make yourself sick.

*

THE NOBLEMAN: There is nothing on earth
more exquisite than a bonny book, with
well-placed columns of rich black writing
in beautiful borders, and illuminated

pictures cunningly inset. But nowadays, instead of looking at books, people read them. A book might as well be one of those orders for bacon and bran.

*

WARWICK: I apologize to you for the word... It does not mean in England what it does in France. In your language traitor means betrayer: one who is perfidious, treacherous, unfaithful, disloyal. In our country it means simply one who is not wholly devoted to our English interests.

*

CAUCHON: Some men are born kings; and some are born statesmen. The two are seldom the same.

*

DUNOIS: Do you expect stupid people to love you for shewing them up? Do blundering old military dug-outs love the successful young captains who supersede them? Do ambitious politicians love the climbers who take the front seats from them?

*

KING CHARLES: I would not go through that [*coronation*] again to be emperor of the sun and moon. The weight of those robes! I thought I should have dropped when they loaded that crown on to me. And the famous holy oil they talked about so much was rancid – phew!

*

JOAN: You promised me my life; but you lied... You think that life is nothing but not being stone dead. It is not the bread and water I fear... Bread has no sorrow for me and water no affliction. But to shut me from the light of the sky and the sight of the fields and the flowers... to make me breathe foul damp darkness... I could do without my warhorse; I could drag about in a skirt... if only I could still hear the wind in the trees, the larks in the sunshine, the young lambs crying through the healthy frost... But without these things I cannot live: and by your wanting to take them away from me, or from any human creature, I know that your counsel is of the devil, and that mine is of God.

*

THE GENTLEMAN: I have been requested by the temporal authorities of France to mention that the multiplication of public statues to the Maid threatens to become an obstruction to traffic.

NOTE ON THE TEXTS

These extracts are taken from the first editions of plays, which were first published between 1914 and 1924 (see over). Shaw took great care over what many might consider minutiae of the editorial process, and had strong views on punctuation, spelling and typography. As such, this edition strives to replicate his approach – his lack of italics for publications and ships, and of apostrophes in contractions, which he considered unsightly (e.g. 'doesnt', 'isnt'), his unusual variant spellings (such as 'Shakespear' and 'shew') and his preference for American spellings (e.g. the '-ize' suffix) – in order to preserve the original reading experience. In some instances, spelling, punctuation and grammar have been silently corrected to make the text more appealing to the modern reader. The act each quote is taken from is given afterwards, except for one-act plays. In some instances short stage notes immediately following the speaker's name, where not relevant to the quote, have been elided. Omissions are marked with ellipses, except from where words have been omitted from the start of quotes.

ORIGINAL PUBLICATION DATES

OF THE PLAYS

1914   *Misalliance*

1914   *The Dark Lady of the Sonnets*

1914   *Fanny's First Play*

1916   *Androcles and the Lion*

1916   *Overruled*

1916   *Pygmalion*

1919   *Heartbreak House*

1919   *Great Catherine*

1919   *O'Flaherty V.C.*

1919   *The Inca of Perusalem*

1919   *Augustus Does His Bit*

1919   *Annajanska, the Bolshevik Empress*

1921   *Back to Methuselah*

1924   *Saint Joan*

ALSO AVAILABLE BY BERNARD SHAW
FROM RENARD PRESS

The life of fifteenth-century heroine Joan of Arc is the stuff of legend, and her cruel death (burnt at the stake aged just nineteen) led to her being declared a martyr, granting her an extraordinary legacy.

Following her canonisation in 1920, and against a history of overly romanticised retellings of the story, Bernard Shaw put pen to paper to give a more accurate account, without resorting to demonising her persecutors; as he writes in his preface, 'there are no villains in the piece'.

It was an immediate success, securing him the Nobel Prize for Literature, although critics were initially divided by this frank approach – T.S. Eliot was outraged, saying, 'instead of the saint or the strumpet of the legends… he has turned her into a great middle-class reformer.' Nonetheless – or perhaps even because of this controversy – *Saint Joan* is considered one of Shaw's finest and most important plays.

This edition has an introduction by Simon Mundy, who has spent several years as Vice-President of PEN International's Writers for Peace Committee, and extensive explanatory notes.

ISBN: 9781913724658
Paperback • £7.99 • 256pp

WWW.RENARDPRESS.COM

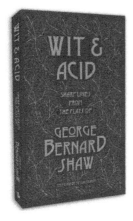

'If you want to tell people the truth, make them laugh, otherwise they'll kill you.'

One of the most prolific and respected playwrights of the twentieth century, Bernard Shaw's legacy shows no signs of waning, and his beautifully written plays, laced with wry wit and invective alike, have seen countless performances over the years, their finest lines paraded in literary conversation and review.

Meticulously selected by Simon Mundy, the *Wit and Acid* series collects the sharpest lines from Shaw's oeuvre in small neat volumes, allowing the reader to sample some of the very best barbs and one-liners the twentieth century has to offer, and this, the first volume, covers lines from the great writer's works published up to 1911.

'He was a Tolstoy with jokes, a modern Dr Johnson, a universal genius who on his own modest reckoning put even Shakespeare in the shade.'
The Independent

ISBN: 9781804470114
Paperback • £6.99 • 88pp